Y0-BPZ-629

A
FLASH
OF
SWALLOWS

A FLASH OF SWALLOWS

new poems by

William Christopher Stevens

DROKE HOUSE, *Publishers*

ANDERSON, S. C.

8375-6734-3

A FLASH OF SWALLOWS
Copyright ©1969 by DROKE HOUSE, Publishers

All Rights Reserved

No part of this book may be reproduced or transmitted in any form whatsoever, or by any means, electronic or mechanical, including photocopying, or by any information storage or retrieval system, without permission in writing from the publisher.

FIRST EDITION

Standard Book Number: 8375-6734-3

Library of Congress Catalog Card Number: 69-14346

Published by DROKE HOUSE, Publishers
1109 S. Main St.
Anderson, South Carolina

MANUFACTURED IN THE UNITED STATES OF AMERICA

Book Design by Lewis N. Schilling, Jr.

The Poetry of William Christopher Stevens

The phrase *split personality,* for no truly logical reason, suggests a splitting into two equal halves. The work of W. C. Stevens, one of the better known Australian poets, reveals that an artistic personality, at least, can be split up into far more than two parts. There can be no question but that Stevens has several voices, several quite distinct styles. To some extent, of course, this is true of all interesting poets; the difference in Stevens pertains to degree. Among his separate voices are the ironic, the tender, the religious, the agnostic, the solemn, the playful, the crystal-clear, the ambiguous, the lyrical, the matter-of-fact, the bitter, the wise, the — one could go on almost ad infinitum, so many separate poses does Stevens strike.

The word *poses* may be unfairly chosen, for profound sincerity is fundamental to Stevens' poetic position. But the fact remains that he somehow presents himself to society as a one-man crowd, now speaking in strident urgency, now in delicate lyricism, now in moral outrage, now in old-fashioned warmth. It is as if he realizes that there is no universal audience prepared to embrace all poetic styles and consequently has decided to appear in various guises so as to reach the largest possible listenership.

Certainly Stevens is even more widely listened to than read since he appears frequently on Australian television and radio to read his works.

There is a photographic element in Stevens' imagery, I think, that may have some connection with his television experience. He will introduce a line that takes a long-shot view and then in the next instant zoom in for an incredibly tight close-up, of the sort associated with modern cinematic techniques. Such a close-up "shot," for example, would be the lines from *Seeing*:

> Your tongue curves wet and up and
>   makes the *luh* that *love* begins with
>   then your upper teeth hiss warmly,
>   effly
> on your lower lip . . .

Elsewhere Mr. Stevens frankly states:

> A poem
> Is a photograph of words
> Designed as well
> As any Kodak snap
> Some tender spot of time
> To thus entrap . . .

but characteristically emphasizes that poems, like photographs are secondary, not primary, reality.

> . . . a juicy apple sucked and bitten
> means more than verse
> about an apple written.

6

Another identifying mark of the poet's style is in his insight that nature's roots are sunk in time as well as space. Where most poets would be content to *describe* a stand of silent trees on an Autumn afternoon Stevens observes:

> There is an ageless waft of patience in
> trees
> That lends a strange dimension to this
> silence.
> They can and will outwait us.
> When the fruiting seed of spirit cracks
> the body's husk
> Then worms have at us first
> But in the end green trees and grass
> Eat worms and us as well as all proud
> lions.

Apparently it is impossible to analyze a poetic style without reference to the influence of predecessors and peers. But precisely because of the variety of mode that characterizes Stevens' work, it is difficult to locate him in the constellation of modern English-language verse. That he has been influenced by I. R. Jefferson is, of course, clear. One can say, however, that the influence is minor, productive and even, in a sense, liberating. Certainly there are few modern poets who have a greater, more lubricated ease of expression than Jefferson. On the other side of the coin, Stevens has never succumbed to Jefferson's occasional lapses into a lush, Byzantine inscrutability – an almost impenetrable ambiguity, the more puzzling in that it is at odds with the general direction of his work, which is towards clarity, tautness and economy.

In his 1959 review of *Spiders and Sparrows* Leigh Dunsmuir argued – by no means convincingly – that it was precisely in Jefferson's most densely turgid passages that the poet was making his most significant utterances. Certainly the same could never be said of Stevens. What is fundamental to his philosophy is stated with the greatest clarity.

With those who see similarities between Stevens' works and that of his illustrious countryman, A. D. Hope, I share no understanding. Even beyond the primary distinction, so obvious it scarcely requires stating, that Hope restricts himself almost entirely to traditional forms – there is, or so it seems to me, a brazenness, an abrasive modernity to Stevens' tone that is – for better or worse – quite lacking in Hope.

The poet's Australian admirers, knowing that he has a vigorous following throughout the United Kingdom, find it difficult to understand that he is relatively unknown in the United States. The explanation is simplicity itself: Stevens has never been published here, largely perhaps because of a bias against Australian poets on the part of American publishers. One scarcely breaks even on the works of major American poets, goes the argument. Why bother to publish those of foreign authors for whom there is no ready audience?

To properly introduce himself to his new audience Stevens has included in this new collection a group of poems growing out of specifically American experiences. Though his ties here are tenuous they do exist. One of his sons attends college in Colorado and Stevens himself has twice visited the states, once in 1957, merely as a tourist, and again in 1961 as participant in a world conference at San Francisco on the theme of International Law.

Australian poetry generally has a traditional, formal coloration that may explain the general lack of enthusiasm for it on the part of American publishers in a day when the dominant American tone is modern, experimental and still considerably Poundian. While paying due obeisance to the conservative forms, Stevens more frequently sounds a note that one feels will easily conform to American prejudices.

— M. L. Silver.

Why Tears Are Salt

Bellow, beloved, muffled like
   the gray-green sea beasts
That hugely lunge and
     swoop in my
     creative dreams
And too through
     vasty submarine perspectives.

Bellow, squeal, sweat and tumble.
It's the only exercise you're getting
   lately.

It took a mighty heave to lift us —
   hail hail the gang's all here —
up out of the sea, and we were
    not, apparently, fully equal to
      the task,
For we brought brine and tangle
    with us, salt to sweat out
in our tortured moments, sorrow juice from eyes
   betraying that
Some smiles are more disguise.

Even now after ten million years — we've watery
   dreams.

A Quiet Afternoon of Waiting

Tick and, as they put it, *tock*
At least so states the stately clock.
Soft sounds abound this afternoon,
Clicks, creaks, pale drippings, quiet thuds and sighs.
Outside, a forest drowned in silence
Rippled by sound pebbles tossed
From the gullet of a loon.

Under the earth's moist dark the roots
Of these and all trees everywhere
Join hands. An interlocking
Web of silent tendons there.
Conspirators that bribe with nuts and fruits.

There is an ageless waft of patience in trees
That lends a strange dimension to this silence.
They can and will outwait us.
When the fruiting seed of spirit cracks the body's
    husk
Then worms have at us first
But in the end green trees and grass
Eat worms and us as well as all proud lions.

Though she may squander profligately fast
Nature's books are balanced at the last.

Weeding Cactus

I attacked the cactus, hacking prickly
knuckles, thickly-sinewed arms, that sprang
   and fought me back, bled pale green blood
   at wounds my blade
   inflicted yet tore my skin
   and stung me badly as a flock of
   cranky wasps.

The giant cactus died, its heart cut out,
roots snapped, limbs chopped by my machete, but
   I, a month after the battle, still
   bear scars. Cat-scratches on my
   wrists and thighs, and high up
   on my arm a rash of angry
   welts. That plant
a million years ago learned how to frighten off
attackers or, if they persisted, make
   them suffer consequences.

I fought
an ancient wisdom.

From Where The Songs?

It seems not very difficult to find
    That source of inspiration in my mind
Whence come these poems, words all strung like
    beads.
    They float up from the cauldron of my needs,
Expressing with a gloss of rhyme or beat,
    Emotion, concept given flesh and heat.

But far more difficult to render clear
Is that mysterious realm from which I hear
    The melodies that rise at times unbidden.
Their genesis may be forever hidden.

There is no effort in their swift creation
Their notes like stars in some found constellation.
    They seem to be delivered more than made
As if one overheard a ghost that played
    In some lost blue dimension without light
Where music fills a wide and endless night.

·I have but to exclude what meets my eyes,
    And close my ears when, not to my surprise,
Rich song in pure harmonic order wrapped,
    Sweet notes like birds in metric cages trapped
    Present themselves to my astonished heart.

The process seems too simple to be art
    Which I had thought required a certain rigor.
    There are, of course, dilemmas that loom bigger
    But few more puzzling, though I've pondered long,
    Than this, the origin of all my song.

My Sons

I fished for souls in the deep can-be void of time
  and drew up singly three, clothed them in flesh,
  prized them, boasted of them, practiced love
    upon them.
But while my back was turned they swam away
not hopelessly beyond my sight, 'tis true, but
  always slipping after that the tattered nets of love.

They still splash close but own themselves.
I readily concede their right to freedom
  but feel their loss as much as if it could
    have been prevented.

When the fourth appeared I looked away the less
  and smiled the more into the waters.

Rocketry

Bursts. Bursts of lightning, bursts of love,
of chrysanthemums' explosion
of the mountain cataract
    the absolutely fat vermillion swell
    of wine freed suddenly;
    of me freed suddenly by
Bursts. Bursts of bubbles in the blood
And of giggles in the dark
And of oh-my-God the heat
That melts the lines of angles
    makes them curves,
That melts the lines of cubes and
    makes them balls
That melts the lines of me and
    makes them loosely intersect
    the lines and curves and balls and
    smoke of you.

I put the ice-cold green and yellow
    melonballs
In here between my teeth and feel
    them burst
And you so close
    the juice runs down your chest.

Visiting My Son

Visiting my son, at school in Colorado:
   Steamboat Springs, we share each
   other and the mountain air, the
father-son embarrassment and love,
   the brash and tumbling creek he
takes me to, high in the hills.

He is an eighteen year old collie-dog,
This fine young man of honey and of bone, he
   and an older brother — we strung together by
   invisible
ropes of love, move up the mountainside.

Bushes tremble, boulders split in the screaming
   silence of the rocky mountain Spring.
We who elsewhere see, smell, feel the brusque
assaulting
   sea that crashes on a pliant coast
assume that this is water's chiefest power.
But truly it is found on inland hills and crags
   where melting snows and clouds, out of
   their gentle softness,
work a fearful force that budges,
   cracks and heaves the mightiest wood and stone.

A lovely chaos blinds and then re-opens eyes afresh
    where water works some Oriental forms out of
    this occidental mass.

At day's end: darkness comes?
    The hell it does. Light goes.
What comes is verbal symbol for the negative.
We sense little but in relation to its opposite. It
    takes hard stone to make us tingle to soft flesh, a
    desert
    to delineate the water, and hatred to make clear
    how rich is love.

California Ocean Cove

Blowing green sweet ripples
    athwart grey whale-belly waves
The fragrant breezes come commingling
    salt and heather in this cove, mixing
gulls and ghosts of fog in this enormous
    azure bowl of golden light.

High, brown blind buffalo of mountains
    sensing the sea, fierce heads lowered,
sink hidden massive legs into the surf and
    underrock.

Endlessly and still, again and ever the water
    rolls on, now molten pearl, crystal, alabaster,
diamond, flashing wanton in the cooling haze-filled
    light of afternoon, splashing with insane abandon
as the ocean scatters treasure ever on the shore
    and for reward receives it back again.

The sea, bunching its muscles, hurls itself in wild
    attack endlessly upon and over through and at
the camel bison grizzly mighty rocks.
    Where there are narrow clefts between clenched
    fists of stone the water alters personality
entirely, no more the placid timeless sea of slow

Pacific reputation
but now a seething screaming roaring mass of currents
  a million separate veins that jostle for position,
twisting, grinding in a deafening sudsy blow of chaos.

  Through the alleys thin the water shoulders
  thunderish
rolling, hissing, rumbling, the close wet sight of it
  enough to wash your eyes and soul.

Off to the holy right one huge mad craggy hump of
rock,
  brown, high as a seven story building, stands
imbedded to the core of earth, awash in gentle surf
  yards from the creamy rootbeer suds that lift and
slosh. An open corridor permits wild waves to crash
  carousing through, shooting spray straight up,
fighting through the narrow passage but at last to
  fan out, simmer down and sink with gentle whisper
in the hillowed sand or stand about in foamy pools
  along the hot beach rim.

  Warm moist breezes nudge the wrapper from a
  Hershey
bar. It comes to rest against my feet. I could
  eat the whole chaotic salty scene.

Cinder

From cracking harsh dominion uck ack
   of stark nuggets something rasps
Sandpaper pain across my liquid eye
   which in due time will humble the
Invader. But try to
   interest me, when ouching 14
Seconds earlier, in that.

We hurt only now, however. Not yesterday and
   never, ever in tomorrow.

Crows

They swim submerged in seas of air
Lazy fins sustain them there,
Black humor in their gaunt unsteadiness.

They cannot dart the swallow's
    sudden slashing line
Nor float lofty and regal
Like the climbing eagle.
They have a clumsy grace
That gives them character.

Let's improve this dreary dusty field of corn
With a scarecrow dressed by Bond Street
    not rag-torn.
These goofy drooping stumblers in air amuse
As now they settle with the twilight's dews
On branch and sward subtracting light
    from sundown
Sample swatches of the black of night to come.

Do they look up at stars as shiny beads
    of fruit they'd like to eat
If they could flap up to a half-moon perch?

Why does a poet singing thrush and wren
    turn up his nose
At crows?

Balance

We are all faithful members of
    the Church of The Great Possibility.
We all keep books that strive to balance
    losses: stab wounds, broken hearts, the monstrous
    born — against the
    credit-side: the pribbling chirp of birds at
    dawn, a breeze in becalmed sails,
    the draught of ice-cold berry-juice on waking
    sour-mouthed.

Grace at meals? Why limit gratitude? Why
    not as well a grace at every breath, at
    every infant's giggle, every suck
    of pine into the nose?

Would such an obligation call, however, for a curse
    at every blow? Damn you, O Lord, and these, Thy
    pains, which
    we receive through Thy carelessness,
    Amen.

Birds

When I lie on my back, staring under
   drowsy lids into the sky, the hawks
      and buzzards,
Taking me for carrion, wheel overhead in
   languid curves and circles, lying
   flatly on the million-layered
   surfaces of summer air.

If I could lie as one day my bones
   will, would these wild birds, I wonder, fall
      at last from their invisible ledge
      of heat,
Knife down and sink their talons in my
   flesh,
      beaks in my eyes? What do they go
      for first, I wonder? Are there parts of
      me especially delicious?

The Great Poets

The great poets have already died
  unsung, who gave us *white*
as a sheet, *I laughed until I almost split*
  my sides, your feet
Are like
  ice.

Each man perhaps created one line
  only, but it stuck
And echoes
  down the ages, leaping mountains,
flying oceans. *You're welcome as the*
  flow'rs in May, butterflies
  in my stomach, hot
as hell, my heart
  was in my mouth, puppy
love. No poet coffee-housing it
  tonight in San Francisco, or accepting
an award in Melbourne, can declare with
  confidence that any shiny beads of words he
    strings together will gleam
as brightly through a thousand years
  as: *pale as a ghost.*

The Sound of Tires

All night through, along Park Avenue,
The braking tires screech
Freezing the heart,
Suspending the activity in a thousand apartments,
Shrieking like Mandrake-roots the size of a
redwood's,
Screaming like the first angel that tumbled into the
pit.

With a horrible high fidelity
The squeal cuts sharp across the consciousness
Of diners with pale teacups poised,
    Sleepers who make of the
        sound a lost heart's weepy plea for love,
        a nightmare monster's close blood-thirsty shout,
    lovers who are either given
        momentary pause or wildly
        cry harmony back to the
        night's intrusive bleat.

The eye winces, the spirit's shoulders hunch.
The sound has strings. In the dark
apartments see the puppets twitch.

Juke Box Investigation

Headless in a cornfield
   in Sangamon County, Illinois,
The dark Italian meat that was de Rosa lay
   among the rustling stalks.

A farm dog found his head and brought it
   to his master
Who, properly, was horrified but soon
   was able to forget.

Some matter of Sicilian vengeance
   more or less routine; the punishment
Fitting the crime as well perhaps as any
   ever does.

One headless stalk among the waving rest,
   One soulless lump of flesh (or, pardon, *two*)
Plaything to lonely dogs,
   Meant as a warning.

de Rosa symbolizes things more terrible
   than those his murderers intended
who now laugh with their children on their knees.

Table Setting: Venice

Glass-throated bell compactly answers glances
as any crust of snow might answer sun
as any desert green respond to rain
    and if exigencies are paler
    than before or ever after
how could plump-groined Rosa smile with the
    brush-strokes rippling pores
    dried in the dull Italian heat?
The atmosphere of genial depravity
    is not measurable by mercury;
    wine-stains on the marble
    can enrich as they besmirch; a twist
of permanence a dash of hate and light
    sans heat or smooth conjuction of
    octagonals. Availability's the thing
and truly it's the level seeks the water.
Pull a yellow ribbon, see what falls,
pluck at the fringes, ravel warp and woof
    to line a lizard's nest. Glitter
    darkly glass anatomy and dare rebel
    if vomiting the spectrum; Leonardo
    didn't wear dark glasses.

St. Hubris

Saints do not believe in themselves but doubt
    themselves.
One rose cannot inspire another.
What ends the beauty of a widening set of ripples is
    the equal beauty of this pool's rock edge.

Beyond my window tremble bright red berry-beads
    that stuff my eye
But would be poison to my tongue.

Some swords and guns are beautiful, and
    even color-slides of cancer cells
        show reds and blues and lavenders
        as bold as those of sunsets
        in the Arizona hills.

The sparrows all lie dead in time that had that
    eye upon them. Perhaps his eye
is also on the worms that hunt
    among the dusty feathers.

Seeing

I must sometime look through a microscope
   and telescope at you.
For else my eyes unaided can not see
   enough to match what something
   in me knows.
It may be yet a million years
   before we sluggard creatures
   forge the words
   to match what something in me knows
   about the – oh, the veins
   beneath your tongue, I don't care.

Could you be bad, I wonder?
Could half a century with you
Be as a micro-second of the ultimate?
Your tongue curves wet and up and
   makes the *luh* that *love* begins with
   then your upper teeth hiss warmly, effly
   on your lower lip and are we
   any wiser for the exercise?

See us in the mirror making love.

If I Died

I would not care much if I died
    except
that there are poems I shall not have time
    to read
And rivers I shall not have time to bathe in,
That there are stars beyond my power of sight
Lost blue seas I shall never sail,
Lips never kissed
And morning chimes in sunny cities I shall not
    awake in.

This is the only reason to fear death
That far too much of life is left unlived,
That certain symphonies will go unheard,
Some mountain snows will melt before one sees them.

Whatever's left when I decay
Will be, I promise you, a mighty
    bursting wild desire.

Observation

I will observe as much as possible, conclude as little
    as I can. Resist
        lustful temptations to make sense, to
        see significance, to draw a moral, base
        a sermon. I will
Let the universal nature — speak? No, for there
    I go assuming I am brushed by the
black batwing of meaning. No, I will give rein
    to nose, to eye, to early-warning system of my
    skin,
Be not the master or philosopher but humble
    servant, even unresisting canvas, of the butterflies
    and pebbles, of breathy pines, that they
    may paint upon my soul the ultra-modernistic
    art that yet sinks roots into the day before
        eternity began.

Vestigial Characteristics

Through certain deep Kentucky caves,
Black as a bat's liver,
There murmurs a mysterious river
Deeper than Hades' graves.

Men have tremblingly descended,
Dry-mouthed by lamp dint,
Below the root of the mint
Where past and now are blended

And found there thriving eyeless fish
That sighted were in prehistoric days,
But never dreamed of heaven's rays
And so forgot the optic wish.

There is a lesson in these holes:
Unless we pay our nature's debt
To godliness there yet
May come a race of men sans souls.

The Hammock

From a catalogue I bought a hammock.
No pair of trees stand close enough
    together on my land
To sling it in the air. Well-knowing this I
    bought it anyway
and have enjoyed it in a sense, have
    floated cradled in its stringy arms in some
    strange way, indeed almost remember
    doing so, sipping lemonade
        above the green.

I have a confidence
    the future will somehow bring trees together for
    me.

How Can We Love The World?

How can we love the world
Who stiffen in the close proximity
　　of crowded elevators?
How can we love all others
　　as ourselves who hate ourselves?
Wounds are struck like lightning but
　　cut flesh assembles slowly as stalagmites
　　　　(stalactites?)
The same stupidity confuses them
That makes me less than God.

Jolly jolly red like holly
　　jelly beans
In bright green Easter paper nested,
Red and beads of lavender
That make the young eye giggle
Tempt us far too much and bring
　　about therefore their own destruction.

It's a blessed thing that rubies, pearls have
　　no taste
Or else one sense would overpow'r another
The wealthy stout would suck their jewels.

The trick's in learning to be sensitive

enough but not, oh God, no never
   to the point where
We'd see everything in honest focus
For the jails, orphanages, the
   hospitals and jungle traps, hot
   jaws of sharks
Are much too full for that.

We'd weep such tears as then would turn
   the desert world to green and northern
   fields to ice.

There must be creatures, selves or souls
   on other planets
Qualified to weep for us who sympathize
   not quite enough to
   match the pain of mothers' bearing monsters
Or seeing perfect children turned to
   monstrous shapes on filthy fields of war.

As I Was Saying To St. Ives

Honey, swockey Molly Pons
    or Lily Pons
She's lovely, she's engaged
And therefore you can't see her now.
And why should juice betray us?

It's there or isn't there
    to lubricate, digest, or culminate.

Yes, Howard Culmin (1860-1912)
Invented Culminate, the hot
    explosive made of tears
    and sweat from lonely telephones
    Touched often in the empty summer night.

Ah. Why is all the best the
    saddest part of all?
The wound's made in a bee's-wings' flicker
But the healing takes a ton of time.

The Chinese bound the feet
    And what bind we
    if we are failing to perceive
There's just no physics, chemistry
    for love?

or, rather, such there is but
what's within the test tube
Undergoes a magic change of name.

See us in the mirror — yes, again —
    a not-disgusting good *menage a quatre.*
Two pairs of naked twins.
I'd like to kiss you some day in
    a house of mirrors
So in one reflective* moment I
    could see you an infinity
    of times.

*(Laugh it up. Or get it up just any way you can.)

Incense and Crackling Bells

A case of halitosis in my neighbor:
    quite enough to overwhelm
The Francis of Assisi urge this afternoon, so slender
    is the reed of virtue. Our Father,
who probably art in heaven, hallowed be
    Thy name, whatever it turns out to be. Thy
kingdom come, though come as a surprise it will.

Thy will be done, but who would recognize it
    if it were? On earth as it is in heaven,
from whence no witness has as yet returned. Give
    us this day our daily bread; last
Thursday, for example, when the bloated bellies
    of Biafra cracked like rotten melons
in the summer sun. Forgive our debts — if
    those insisting that the word is *trespasses*
Will take their hands off the throats of those who
    favor *debts* — as we forgive our debtors,
And other shifty bastards, who trespass against us.

For tyrone is the power and the gloryosky, Zero,
    for ever endeavor ah-hah. No, amigo,
Not a bit of heresy but merely an attempt to
    cut crust off some ancient words.
But don't throw all that crust away. It may
    be the best part.

Midwestern Summer Night

This night each starry stab of light
   across the river trails a wriggling
     snake of silver
In the water.

A distant sadly comic saxophone
   cries faintly in the black and sultry summer
   mystery
Who . . . stole my heart away?
   Who . . . An old piano mingles soft
   into the blessed Iowa breeze,
Crickets chirp and rasp a song as your
   slow breathing in my ear blends with
   the heat, the scent of dewy clover and
   the not quite heard strum buzz of stars.

It is a night for nakedness
   of soul.

A Photograph of Words

A poem
Is a photograph
Of words
Designed as well
As any Kodak snap
Some tender spot of time
To thus entrap.

Poetry, for all
The beauty of the best of it,
Is, like the picture, secondary not the
Prime reality. Poems
Are signs and arrows leading
Us to what is
Fundamental. A juicy apple sucked and bitten
Means more than verse
About an apple written.

The Seven Profitable Sins

The after-dinner cookie, two-holed, sneering
   at me insolently, like a pig's nose,
   Cried gluttony, that capital sin the
   encouragement of which is the chief business
    of our advertisers.

But the other once-atrocities-now-pecadillos
   — or are they virtues? — are not overlooked.
The scarlet close-ups of lipsticks and Jello,
   mountain-strata chocolate-cakes that
   bring your hungry eye right to the saucer's edge
   — devil's food indeed — the power-mowers,
   gold liquers, the perfumed breasts and
   nyloned thighs, ICBM's, all sell, really,
Pride, covetousness, lust, anger, gluttony, envy
   sloth.

I never knew until arriving here, and would have
   marvelled to suppose, that God is an American
   patriot.

The red blood of Christ, His white body, against the
   blue Good Friday sky.

Reality

I see reality, now and then, out of the corner of
   my eye, as if a swallow had flashed overhead,
And, turning with the hope of seeing it directly,
Find it gone or fast disguised.

A word, a glance, a lightning-glimpse of
   stockinged thigh,
   smiling insult,
Sharply focused, fully understood, but
   then, when I attempt a close inspection,
Something vanishes, perhaps the essence. Oh, wise
indeed
   am I, in some far corner of my mind to which
   I have as yet no voluntary access.

The Way Back

These God-damned marks on paper:
   tatters, scraps tossed back along
   the path is all they are
So I'll be able now or soon or late
To find my way back to —
Back to?

Ah, now I've done it,
Let the wind get at them, blow
   them here and there
Or dropped them else too seldom on the honey earth
So all the space between defeats me now.

I'm a marvelous computer but can
   I program myself?
A word like garter-belt's enough
   to start a throb and hum.
We feed each other words, love, you
   and I
While at the rounded metal corners where
   we meet the floor
Are those drops oil or blood?

Roundelay

When your hair has turned to henna
Quoth the raven at Ravena,
When your hair has turned to silver
And your silver's turned to hair,
Come a ti-yi-yipee
Eat your peanut-butter, Skippy,
By the livin' maid that's got you
You're a dirty little snot, you,
And if I should wake before I die
I pray the Lord my old school tie.
If I should die before I wake
I hope it's from a belly-ache.
If I should laugh before I cry
Then somewhere in the buy-and-buy
A cheer:
All right, gang! Let's make it a big locomotive!
On your feet!

And we stand and silently cheer
As we silently stand and pray,
   heads down,
A posture from which eyes may
   Shyly look at breasts.

The Miller To His Mate

We've got to start in planning now,
    this afternoon, hot clover notwithstanding,
For a happy marriage. Oh, not yours and
    mine,
But for our grandson's grandsons'. Anything
    begun a second after will be
    much too little and too late.

God help us, no one ever planned for
    yours and mine
So daily now we fight our way
    through puppet strings invisible
    that make this sturdy web
    stretched taut and tense
To trap and kill the random flies
    of happiness.

In A Glass Darkly

The electric razor has a razor's edge.
Safety in numbers, said the
   Harlem bagman
Sorry, wrong number, said the
   Fifth Commandment to the Sixth.

A resolution to amend the Decologue
   was introduced by Sen. Sen-sen
   yesterday, according to a usually
ridiculous source.

A burst of fireworks seen in a
   mirror leaves no cracks or streaks of light
   except on memory, no seven
   years bad luck, no
      matter.

Anti-matter. What's the matter, Auntie?
Careful, don't you make light of
   my jokes or else, by God,
I'll take my clown's mask off
   And scare you all to death
   except for those still willing
      to embrace me.

Florentine Light

Could Da Vinci have been
   a late sleeper? I see
   that golden light but
only in the afternoon. Frenchmen
   were up earlier, I think. Let's
ask a blind man to paint
   what he sees.

Flying

When I was very young there was a time
I thought that I could fly.
I knew, of course, that as of any given moment
My feet were hopelessly ground-glued
And yet it seemed there'd been a time
Not long before
When naturally as any bird or ghost
I'd willed myself up suavely into air
And caught my breath and flown (rather low
So as not to fight with fear as well as gravity)
About the yard behind our building.

I told a friend about it all one time.
He laughed, quite understandably. Indeed
I had to laugh myself, but once I'd laughed
I found I couldn't fly at all. Then
Or ever.

View From A DC-7

From ten thousand feet
   the ragged, pale, flat-bottomed clouds
lying level at four thousand
Float with a magic
We forgot to marvel at a billion years
   ago.

Only up here now
Does it seem like a trick again

Looking down we peer
into the pure transparent sea
That shelves the vapors
Seeing, far beneath its
   surface,
The green-robed Alleghenies
The flat bed of Ohio
And now at last Atlantis: Chicago

Pain

The time the handle of an axe
　　cracked hard across my face
I bled, of course, and sat down and
　　all that, but then my friends
　　rushed in and held me, deeply
　　cared, feared for me, wondered
　　if my eyes were well.

The strangest sense of comfort and of
　　peace, like that induced by
　　codeine, took me up into its arms.

What memory was this? What physical
　　response evoked by pain, close
　　followed by concern? It was a form
　　of beauty — that I know — which has a
　　way of bubbling up when least expected.

Summer Storm

The morning's soul leans tiredly on the
    parchment shades, soft-billowing
And as in woodlands tiny creatures scamper
    at the wolf's footfall
Small paper tatters hustle at the storm's approach
    down in the street.

The breeze frets where the — Oh! The lightning
    crackled over Brooklyn.
Now the displaced peasants cross themselves
    and wipe the spattered sills.

There's white against the lower lids of eyes
    and sly appreciation now of roofs.
The storm breaks angrily and ancient gods
    roam Central Park
The pigeon's crusts lie soaked, the buried
    worm lifts up its thoughts
and the same water that has rained since time began
    falls knowingly, with gravity familiar.

Summer Storm

The heavens shout a gutteral thunder-clap
    and in the instant (statisticians)
Twenty-two million adrenal glands (divide
    by two) pump juice
That makes men turn, if chemically, to God
    as other juices make them turn to other things.

Joints ache and blood knows something's
    going on, for nature's one
And all the city is aslosh with juice
    and steam.

The motorists weaving through the park
    sniff deeply at the moist-earth smell,
their cells sifting among the gas exhaust
    for farm-fresh country scents.

Rain rain go away the children sing
    not meaning it
But go away it does and too as bidden it
    returns another day.

Poplar Tree

a
pin
sharp,
feather
pointed
graceful
poplar-tree
swayed lightly
at the nudging of
flirtatious breezes,
danced delicately in the
yellow morning light that
put a hazy canvas under
neath the girlish limbs
and, seen from where
I lay upon the
grass, seemed
to be tickling
clouds. Unseen
mad sparrows
in the tree
top giggled,
fluttered,
gossiped
in the
treetop
keeping
secrets
from me
that I
longed
to hear
as I
lay
on
a
hill beneath the tree and peered up through the leaves.

Terrace Tree

Lone tree, poised delicately above Park Avenue,
Do you get dizzy on the 19th floor? Of all
the stupid questions.

Sequoia-high but rooted in a box
Wind-swept but tap-watered
Sun-drenched, but mulched and pampered
Ambivalent creature, forced to share frustrations with
your master,
Why not surprise him? Send a leaf
Fluttering to his table at 21;
Tell him you too have developed an ulcer.
Imagine!
Leonard Lyons will be sure to mention your name.

Enemies

Fire and ice are enemies;
No sermons can unite them.

I
A large block of ice
Attacked by a small fire
Will wash the flame to nothingness

II
A small block of ice
Attacked by a large fire
Will die in wisps of steam.

III
Or they can be so finely balanced
that they cosign
a suicide pact.

I and II are preferable to III
It shows poor breeding to
    return a gift.

Day On The Sound

The sails are so numerous this morning
Distance single-files them,
Makes Long Island the inverted
   jawbone of a shark
Which, though long dead, gleams
   with jagged youthful teeth.

The Limits of Compassion

I can not suffer for you.
You must do it all yourself.
Unless, of course, I self-inflict
    the wound you've just sustained,
See my wife faithless just as
    yours has been
Or have my tooth extracted after yours.
And even then the two would have to
    happen simultaneously
And even then our pain-thresholds
    might vary
And even then semantic barriers block the way
    to common understanding.
To that extent we live on separate planets.

The diving-board, to me, looks only
    four feet from the water
But you're not in your feet; you're up
    behind your eyes
And that is six feet more so you're ten
    feet above the water;
For all of me you're very much alone.

Genius Before Its Time

Who were the poets
    before Adam knew of words?
The men who sniffed
    at violets their fellows had ignored or crushed, the
Brutes who yet could notice fuzz
    on peaches,
smile at clouds or spy
    the green geometry of ferns.

How many Beethovens died in those endless
    epochs before song? How many Caesars
    ruled the subjects of one hut, da Vincis scribbled
    on prehistoric desert sand or
    Freuds fought witch-doctors?

Sufficient unto the eon is the beauty
    thereof. A monumental genius or
    two must surely walk among us
    now unknown because their instruments
    will not be manufactured till we
        make a strange device of Martian metal,
        a chip of some eternity from now.

Right and Wrong

The theory of the infinity of error:
There is only one right answer to the
question: How much are two
   and two, but there
Is no limit to the number of
wrong answers. One of them, for
example, is 317. Another is
egg-salad sandwich and I
dare say that part of it had not
even occurred to you.

A Line Of Dunces

A line of dunces
embedded in the asphalt street
only their pointed hats
showing coned above the surface.

They shyly hulk below
giggling in concrete as the
Bored line-painters up above go
quietly about their business.

1956: Summer, New York

Inventory, city man:
   Jaguar, *Harper's,* camera-case,
   Checkered vest and bearded face.

   Though the asphalt stretches warm
   you remain in uniform.

   Given to wearing jaunty caps
   off you speed, upstate perhaps,

   To mild rendezvous with fate
   Drunk at 7, dine at 8.

   Say what brighter men have said,
   Snub your wife and go to bed.

   Aren't you a pretty dish
     to set before a king?

The Lovely Colors of the War

How lovely is the shiny Christmas trinket red
    of children's guts
Laced gracefully against the green
    of jungle fronds.
How pink the brilliant patch of flame-seared
    flesh appears
In contrast with the tattered dark
    pyjama. How white the splintered bone.

How clear the hot pig-squeal of panic rings
    against the sudden quiet of this village.
How black the wings of death that
    beat against these wild, reproachful eyes,
How fire-truck scarlet all these pools
    of hot civilian blood
Against the yellow straw, the tan bamboo.

How bitter sour the stink of crappy death, of
    sweat wrung out by fear. How slippery
The feel of once sweet skin now blistered,
hamburgered, each
    quivering nerve
Sinking needles in the mind so
    deep they fall below the soul and
down into the animal.

How blue the heaven that impartially
    looks down.

Desire

I want to run as fast as
   I can, and leave the ground
And jump into your mind.
   And wildly but methodically explore
The vast entirety of you. The past,
   The endless crossroads of the present.
The future will take care of itself
   if we are hand in hand.

Poem For Children

The only simple thing we know
Is that there's nothing simple.
The moist meat computer (who
    says *watch out for moisture when*
      you're plugged in?) that
throbs in my skull, projects
itself, at end, only to the cloud high
    barriers of the three
    pairs of non-possibles: Space,
Time and God.

A trio of these alternatives, you
    understand, are more than
mutually exclusive; they're absurd
    as snowballs shoveled into furnaces.

A: Space either *ends* (which is
    impossible) or *doesn't* (which is silly)
B: Time either starts-ends (once
    again, impossible) or *doesn't* (laugh, I
    thought I'd bust
      a gut)
C: God either *is* (preposterous, for the
    old, historic reasons) or *isn't* (which
    is hardly more acceptable mathematically. It

leaves a universe of evidence just not
accounted for).

So circle right and form a star
Duck for the oyster; there you are
Swing your lady to and fro
Chicken in the bread-pan pickin' up the dough.

Foote and Cone and Belding, too
To hell with *Crest*, it's *love* for you.
You've sold gluttony and greed
When it's charity we need.
You've sold things so very well;
Sell us man or here comes hell.

Experiment

Let's try
writing a poem
on a piece of colored stock.

Get paper of various colors,
dab it with several scents.

Yellow tea-rose for a poem
on a California morning
golden-misted and wet-earth smelling,
with snail tracks drying glassily on the rocks.

Azure floral paper for a verse
about a Paris night

But if we cannot read it to a blind man
and make him tingle
it isn't any good.

Selective Sensitivity

How can I possibly love
   the faces of dogs
as much as I do?
Love them, I mean, with
   that leap of smile
in the heart that lovers feel
   in the most gloriously blazing
spring of passion.

What misplugged circuitry
   in my medulla is responsible
for this, that while brown
   infants gasp and stare
dying in the world's gutters
   I love dogs' mouths and eyes.

The Crowded Board

When you and I sit down to dine
    supposedly alone
There sit beside, behind us
    ghostly pairs and fours and eights, etc.
of ancestors, some quite compatible
    but others not.

No word I drop escapes lightning
    analysis by those grim
visitors from back along the misted
    stream of your germ plasm.
No facial tic of yours but is observed
    by those mixed savages and gentlefolk
who stare at you across my brow.

It is a wonder we know
    any peace.

Models

The models posing
truly living *moving* pictures, as
   the saying goes.

Their funny poses cute but sexless
little prissy girls, their
   blank silurian eyes
that are for looking at
   not seeing with.

Changes

The sins that we commit at twelve
At thirty are washed clear
By boredom more than virtue

    Observe how John's not tempted
      by his wife
    While Howard is.

Our sins are chosen for us
Like our food and clothing
    when as children we but
    plastically receive.

What We Call Billy

We call Billy Billy
And William, The Conqueror
And Kaiser Bill and, when he is
    wearing a yellow suit:
Lemon Drop.
And Billy The Kid and Billy-Boy
And Honey-Boy
And Golden Boy
And Sunny Jim
And Laylio Boy because he pronounces
    radio *laylio*
And we call him Sweet William
    and Just My Bill
And My Boy Bill
And Bill-bill and Willy-Nilly
And Zip, The Chimp
And Muggady-Wump.

Soon it must stop.

Boy in the Morning

Looking at the world sideways he
lay waking

The flowered cotton curtains fluttered cooly
as he yawned,
looking up under the skirt
of the morning.

Soft perfume from the park
and sunlight gently wrapped in mist
and he lying flirting with
the morning.

Junior

Like Frankenstein
The nameless monster
Man of many parts
Whom people gave his maker's name
Man is called or thought
   as God by some
   idolaters.

Has Heart No Reason

Has heart no reason?
Is there no logic to a love?
Am I condemned to be the sport of skies,
    of charging clouds, of flowers?
How did you hurl sweet hooks into my flesh
    not taking aim?
Why felt I not one warning pain or heard
    one cry?

I am not sovereign. I have been overtaken.
    Gone are all my boundaries
Or merged with yours. I am the kingdom
    of the incomplete
Drunk with beauty, swirling through a mist
    of light and shadow, color,
        sound of breathing
        kisses, eyes, oh eyes.
Relearning now the long-forgotten taste of tears
the desperate part of love
    Abjectly bargaining for moments
    Grateful for a glance
But never, never satisfied by even the
    most gluttonous hours
For I can take sufficient food or drink
But never quite enough of you however much you give.

The warp of human destiny
Is crossed on woof or nature
    forming thus the fright'ning wrack
    on which I hang
    transfixed by love
Counting lost those moments that
    are not spent in your arms or sight.

Sweet fruits of summer that have lain
    upon your tongue; I envy them.
Rich symphonies you've heard that I shall
    never hear disturb my peace
For what is past is gone
And what's to come's unsure
    And I can not retard the present moments
    I'd like.
Oh, I would stop the universe some now or
    then and spend
    huge chunks of time in one position or another
    with you, my tender love.
Perhaps a thousand years on one small kiss
    I'd spend before continuing on
    To warm embraces, promises, and dreams.

Old Themes and New

They walk in space now, held by
    umbilical or puppet strings against the
dazzling blue bowling ball of distant earth,
    and here I hang composing
    thoughts of same old
pine-needle and rose.

Why not a poetry of hardware? The stained-glass light
of
    candles seen through rosy wine
is no more beautiful inherently than that
    wild light that blasts the alabaster
pillar up into the silent scream of space.

Lament

Lament
how swiftly
wonders become commonplace
And, worse by far,
how wonder lying at
the nut-heart of the commonplace
lies somewhere just beneath
the spectrum
of our sensitivity.

The Oriental Salutation: You Matter

You matter. You are important. Not only to yourself
    or to adoring me
But to the universe. And that is where the wonder of
    your love strikes fire like lightning.
The thing I hold in arms when I hold you
    is quite the highest thing of all, sans God,
For I do not believe in angels.
    I believe in you.

More than your name, more than your image
    in my heart are you
And though we loved a million years still I could not
    explore the endless space of you.
Please, take my hand, and lead me to your inner
    self. Pray introduce me to your fears
    and needs, for nothing can be helped that
    hides itself.
And nothing need withdraw from me that is a part of
    you. Oh, I may sing the carmine of your lips
    but really it's the red and silent scream
    your nightmare heart conjures that I would know.

I've heard you whimpering by night and stood
    helpless ashore while you sank in a
    sea of dreams. Morning brought your body

floating up.
I held you close but overflowed with love that ran
     like molten gold, splashed through the present
     to the future, past, and will not satisfaction find
Until it fills your every crevice.

Chicago Storm

I saw the snowfall marching.
That's not poetry, it's fact.
Beneath one cloud loose-arching
Hung the lacy cataract,
An orphan snow-storm lonely as a bird
At Woodlawn Avenue and Fifty-third.

I stood and watched it come and go;
Awaited, felt and lost the snow.

I know now snow falls not like prisoned sand
But marches like a spectre on the land.

Three's A Crowd

The best-planned lays of mice and men
Gang aft agley; how long have you
Been a member of the aft-agley gang?

To May, whom it concerns: I dinna ken
That we invited Ken to dinna
And let there be no moaning at the bar
When I pick up the check.

How can I leave thee?
Let me count the ways.
I can do it Sunday, Monday, or Doomsday.
Fee, Fie, Fo, Femme.

Off New Orleans

Off New Orleans they anchor
   the banana boats
From Latin seaports come.

A killing mist is pumped
   into the hold; crew gone,
but watching from across a safe and watery
   distance.

Then — skin creeps! — two
   clouds roll out, one
the murderous gas, rising
   in the warm and salty air, the
other seeming falling oily smoke
   that truly is a crawling
      mass of brute tarantulas.

They ooze, a hairy, frenzied
   wave, escaping one death
For another.

House In The Country

a
thin
feather-wisp
of smoke
lies
faintly
on
the
sky,
shifting
at
the breeze's whim
and
writing
sanskrit
for the
heart to
read.
But
now
the
eye's
drawn down into
the sturdy farm
house standing
silhouetted on
the shadowed arc
of hill that shags up curlily
like a sleeping buffalo's back.
The valley is committed to the
night and stars are due to soon affix
the seal on the bargain. I am a stranger
here and can not know whose life is
indicated by the smoke against the evening
canvas. Is it a lonely hermit or a loving family? Do
aged eyes peer into those smouldering flames seeking
images of times past or does young laughter echo in
that modest house? It is a pity men are born strange
instead of brothers, otherwise I might walk up and
knock upon that paintless door and say I beg your
pardon but I am a brother man and wondered what
your life was like as I came walking up the road along
the valley and so decided to come up and knock and
ask. I do not want to pry or interfere but only to
inquire if you are happy here and if the peace this
house exudes comes from some subtle magic of it's
own or from the glow that lights the hearts that dwell
within. I ask not water or a hand, even, in friendship;
just a word or some small scrap of information or
even just a certain look of eye that indicates some
trust and no suspicion. But the pity is that things are
as they are and if I were to knock upon that door and
ask my blank-faced question I would surely be
suspected of a motive nothing like the one I really
entertain. So I shall keep upon my way along the
valley floor and wish the people of that house a boon
they'll never know. But passing's not a total loss; at
least I'll keep the memory of feather-wisps of smoke
drift-twisted by the piney breeze that wafts soft
summer stars across the mountain sky.

The Crash

To us who nothing knew of war
    the smashed B-25
Smouldering on someone's startled lawn in Phoenix
    made the headlines meaningful.

His eye, perhaps preoccupied with sparrows,
    looked not upon those birds
    that daily screamed and fell
    embraced by gravity's wild arms
    around the globe: looked not
It seems upon this burning shell
    littered with corpses.

But death is not as horrible as
    suffering. Thank God no leather jacket twitched,
    no limb appealed for aid.
    Nothing moved but the curling smoke
Twisting up from the baked-potato blackened
    skulls and arms.

Criticism

When comprehensible to the many I am
    desolate.
When comprehensible to the few, however, I am
    sometimes — re-reading years later —
    incomprehensible to myself, as befits
    perhaps the only truly honest modern poet.

Mirabile ergaton soque est contramos
    funicale recommunicado.

And quite the most marvelous thing
    of all about my work
Are the reviews upon it in the learned
    journals, for who is willing to admit:
I don't know, really, here and there, just what the
hell this
    man is talking about.

Our Fathers

My father died when I was less than two,
And so did yours, as representative of man,
We all have known abandonment, 'tis true,
And since have sifted chaos for a plan.

Our every strength's a weakness, if the rules
That set the game be slightly rearranged.
A thinning line divides wise men from fools;
Both argue that what's destined can be changed.

There are no straight lines for us; all are curved
For all our travel involves going back.
We plant, if not too easily unnerved,
Signs of the past along the future's track.

Point of View

The sun a golden hub
Sending out spokes on the water,
As many spokes as there are looking men
standing quietly on the sand sea-faced.

Each goes directly from the sun
to an eye dazzling its way
beneath the squinted lid.

There are six men.
Six yellow spokes on blue glass
But each
thinks there is one and that it leads
to him.

Only you and I know that
the sun is a golden hub.

LSD

The drug produced one giant spreading web of
   interconnected significance as if
Each word he'd utter were followed by the
   small black daisy of an asterisk
Which, leading the mind's eye to the bottom of a
   vast assumed page, revealed to it there
an endless series of commentaries, every word of which
   was followed by an asterisk, which
   in turn — you see?

Upstanding Citizens:

The Catholic crowds who boasted about Thomas
    Merton as if he were a saint
until they learned that he was liberal, then
judged him with no more recourse to
    standards spiritual.
His crimes? Preferring peace to war, Christ to
Goldwater,
love to paranoia; the ancient gritty failings
    that for two millenia have made the truest
    Christians traitors to the state
    and status quo.

Thursday's Excess

Thursday's excess creates detachment Friday.
Your thighs which Saturday leave me unmoved
Will Sunday irresistible be proved.

While grateful for the turning of the wheel
A part of me rebels at what I feel
For if a mere accumulating juice
That mounts in me as in the growing spruce
Impels, perhaps compels my course and speed
Then what remains of spiritual need?

Baby Talk

Why do we speak to animals in baby-talk? Why, so,
    indeed, to babies? Neither understands the words
    in
        any case, though tone's important.
But what of us does it convey? That we revert
    to our own babyhood and speak — though
    forty-six and hardened —
    as one colt, pup or kitten to another.

The Poet Yawning

Musing on the music of the muse
I'm used, amusedly, to muzzle moos
And yawns unmellifluous mostly
Particularly those that sound most ghostly
The moose moos must be muffled into mews
Though bovine more than feline sounds amuse.

Medieval Song

There's no more I can do
I've done too much already.
   I've baked my heart
   In a loganberry tart
And fed it to my lady.

No more now can I weep.
I've wept too much already.
   My tears filled up
   A golden cup
And I gave it to my lady.

To My Wife On Valentine's Day, 1966

The leaping, screaming jet, burning
    a smoky hole into the pale blue sky
    of morning
Tears me from your arms, your sight,
    your ever-constant warmth
But can not separate me from your
    love
Which, left behind at home, is
    magically with me now
And will be waiting for me when I
    land.

Just so my love for you, a firm
    commitment of the soul
Remains, not subject to the laws of
    space and time.

I go to pay respect to my dead aunt
But more in sympathy to him she
    left behind, desolate by her loss,
Who now must live amongst the relics
    of their love
Unable to observe a tray, a dish, that
    will not speak to him of her.

But I, dear one, need not the spur of
    death
To move me to appreciate the wonder
    you impart
To everything you touch. The artifacts
    selected by your hand
Take from your boundless soul and
    glow with its full golden light.

Old and New

Ah, May was May when I was ten
Heart closer to the ground, and eye-to-eye
   with flowers.
The world shone new, and biting were
   all minty forest scents.
I hoped then truly to put salt on swallow's tails,
Fat random cows had fascination I could feel now
   only at the beasts of Mars.

The wind breathed spirit magic into
   fields of rippled green. I was a part of clouds,
An audience for birds, stern ruler over bugs
   and lover of the sun.

The rains of April fell up then, from moistened
   roots and shaded bowers,
Absorbed into the air by warmer hours.

I sucked the heady mist into my own internal
   branches
A brook meandered through a meadow mumbling
   some soft language I then understood.

Thank God there still are curious ten-year-olds
To look beneath fair Spring's diaphanous folds.

The Green Glen

By the green glen where the white lilies lift
   grandly phallic at the summer air,
In that green dappled glen where in times past
Peasants supposed that fairies dwelt,
You and I in adoration knelt
Prayed thanks for moments that could never last
Then rose and ran with sweet abandon there
Through that cool glen where still fair lilies lift.

Conditioning

We codify our prejudice who live in ignorance.

Would fish, who know deflection of light's rays
Beneath the wave, cool in their shadow world,
Remark, on being lifted up and given lungs for gills,
"Observe how strands from that great globe appear
No longer rightly bent and barely clear
But dazzling to the sight and weirdly straight?"

Furtive Time

I did not note till now
I'd reached the summer of my life.
Spring was such torrent, quake and thunder
That heart was given no time to wonder
At the furtive slipping of the season.
One moment here, then gone, and where the reason?

But theologians strive to weave a reason out of chaos.
If He made us He must need us.
Why then send sharp spurs to bleed us?
Will ever You explain, O Heavenly Prince,
Why difficult it is to change that *if* to *since?*

Fifteen years of marriage

There are Piranhas in our kitchen sink
That clutch bones, flesh, seeds, fruits and all.
There is a mighty giant in these walls
that brings us light and heat, but too can kill.
And endless springs there are beneath our soil
That daily do refresh but so could drown us.

Thus, too, the strong emotion that we feel
For one another can sustain or stifle us.
It is like fire, water, electricity, the
    many forces we require and fear.

Such strength commands respect. We did not
either of us make this wondrous power.
But it is given us, by blessing or blind chance.
Our love, we call it, seeing *our*
and *love* as lacy words on Valentines. No matter
    how we apprehend it, it sustains us.

Sometimes I see the symbols of it, lips and arms
and thighs and breasts. Other times the spirit
of it claims me, lifts me up. Dear woman,
This review is more than cursory.
We've reached another blessed anniversary.